NORWICH CATHEDRAL

G000298652

Above:
The central tower and spire from the south-east.

Left:
The classic view of the cathedral from the south-west corner of the cloister garth.

Contents

Visitors' Guide	opposite
Dean's Welcome	2
History Chart	3
The Ancient Throne	4
The Cathedral's Founder	6
Norwich Cathedral Priory	8
The Cathedral Develops	12
Change and Continuity	16
The Cathedral Today	19

Dean's Welcome

Welcome to Norwich Cathedral.

People have worshipped God in this building ever since its first consecration in 1101. It is a place where you can find faith, joy and peace in Him.

A daily round of worship is offered by the community here, in which visitors are invited to participate. There are many people to welcome you – clergy, voluntary guides, a sister from a Religious Order, vergers and helpers in the Cathedral Shop or at the Welcome Desk.

Please do not rush your visit, but allow time to consider Jesus Christ, without whom this building, for all its glory, would be nothing.

May God give you His blessing.

THE DEAN

History Chart

630 St. Felix, Bishop of the East Angles at Dunwich.

c.673 Removal of the See to Elmham.

1075 Removal of the See to Thetford.

1091 Herbert de Losinga appointed Bishop of Thetford.

1094 Bishop de Losinga removed See to Norwich.

1096 Bishop de Losinga laid foundation stone of the Cathedral.

1101 Consecration of the Cathedral (24 September).

1119 Death of Bishop de Losinga.

1145 Completion of the Cathedral.

1170 Damage by fire.

1272 Severe fire damage.

1297–1430 Rebuilding of cloisters.

1362 Spire blown down. Rebuilding presbytery clerestory.

1463 Spire struck by lightning, resulting in fire.

1480 Presbytery vault and present spire built.

1509 Damage by fire.

1510 Transepts vaulted.

1538 Dissolution of Benedictine Monastery (2 May). Foundation of Dean and Chapter.

1643 Damage to monuments, glass, etc., in Civil War.

1649 Sequestration of the Dean and Chapter.

1660 Restoration of the Dean and Chapter.

1830s Substantial restoration work by Anthony Salvin.

1930 St. Saviour's Chapel built on site of medieval Lady Chapel.

1938 Organ destroyed by fire.

1939 Restoration of organ.

1942 War damage to transepts roofs.

1988 Restoration of St. Catherine's Chapel.

The Ancient Throne

The rarest treasure of Norwich Cathedral is a couple of ancient stones. Heavily calcined by fire, further damaged by exposure to weather for three generations, so that now they bear little resemblance to their original state, they still remain in the place of highest honour in the church, behind the High Altar.

They form all that is left of the Ancient Throne. This is the oldest bishop's throne in use in any English cathedral, and the interest of the fragments themselves is great, as is the tradition behind them.

They have recently been incorporated in a modern restoration, which follows as far as is practicable the design of about 1105. Scholarly re-examinations of them have shown that they were first made at least as far back as the 8th century. The See of East Anglia, fixed at Dunwich in 630 by St. Felix, was divided into two in 673, and a cathedral, probably of timber, was built at North Elmham. It seems to have been replaced early in the 8th century by a stone cathedral, and it was probably for this cathedral that the throne was made. It would have been richly carved with scroll and perhaps with animal or bird forms, and would have stood behind the High Altar.

During the Danish invasion, about 870, Elmham Cathedral was burnt, and its throne badly damaged. The site stood neglected and open to the weather until the Bishopric was restored about 950. Then the cathedral was rebuilt, the fragments recovered, and set up again in the place of honour.

After the Conquest, it was Norman policy to move bishops' sees to important cities, for the bishops' leadership was extending from the spiritual to the secular sphere. The see was therefore moved to Thetford in 1075, and the fragments of the throne were set up there. But Thetford was near Bury St. Edmunds, whose powerful abbot secured from the king and from Pope Hildebrand independence from control by the bishop. At the same time Norwich was rising in importance, so in 1095 the see was moved there. Again the fragments of the throne were moved, and set up in the new cathedral.

The tradition behind the Norwich throne goes back far beyond the 8th century – indeed to the beginning of Christianity itself. The earliest Christian worship took place in borrowed buildings. These may have included the Jewish synagogues, and the pillared halls in which the members of the Mystery cults worshipped. The influence of the Roman Law Court plan, with the judge's throne in the apse, seems clear also. A Mystery hall resembled a Roman Law Court and consisted of a hall with aisles and a semi-

Below: ⑦
The Erpingham window in the presbytery north aisle. A fine collection of medieval Norwich glass from various donors and sources assembled and leaded by Kings, of Norwich, in 1963.

circular apse. Raised on steps in the centre of the apse was the throne, with seats around it, dominating the building as the 'Moses Seat' dominated the synagogue. The description of heavenly worship in *Revelation IV* might seem to suggest a meditation in such a building, with the throne in the apse, the altar before it, the elders around it, and the 'sea of glass', the mosaic pavement, forming the floor.

The Norwich throne remains as a unique survival in England of the primitive plan, practically universal in Christian cathedrals for several centuries. It survives here for the reason that Norwich Cathedral never produced an important saint. Almost every other cathedral did so. Now a saint needed a shrine, to accommodate which with dignity the apse must be replaced by a splendid eastward extension. So Ely had St. Etheldreda, Durham St. Cuthbert, Chichester St. Richard, and Lincoln St. Hugh, each lying in state in a glorious building. Norwich had no such magnificence, but instead it retains its ancient throne. This has recently come to have added significance, as a link between early Christian worship and the modern Liturgical Movement.

The Cathedral's Founder

The founder of Norwich Cathedral was Herbert de Losinga. Possibly a native of Suffolk, he was educated at Fécamp, of which house he became prior. He became abbot of Ramsey, Huntingdonshire, in 1088. He was appointed by William Rufus as Bishop of Thetford in 1091.

The tale is often repeated how Herbert committed simony by purchasing his preferment to the bishopric from Rufus, how he obtained Absolution from the pope (but not the pope whom the king recognised, for there were rival popes at the time), and founded the cathedral as a penance.

In defence of Herbert, who was a holy and generous man in an age of greed and crime, it must be said that the custom of a ruler appointing to high ecclesiastical office and expecting payment for it was of very long standing. It also had the effect of linking the interests of local rulers and church leaders closely together.

Herbert laid the cathedral's foundation stone in 1096, and through his energy and personal generosity the work was so far advanced that its first Consecration took place on 24 September 1101. This is the more remarkable, in that he was also building two of England's largest priory-cum-parish churches: St. Nicholas', at Yarmouth, and St. Margaret's, at King's Lynn. It seems that the whole ground plan was determined from the first, and that portions of the building were pressed forward so rapidly that the native builders were encouraged to follow their own methods, for the west wall of the cloister is of pre-Conquest style, with its small Saxon double-splayed circular windows. The site was already holy ground, for beneath the modern St. Saviour's Chapel at the east end are the foundations of a pre-Conquest chapel, partly re-used as foundations for the Norman chapel for-merly there; there are also indications of a Saxon cemetery nearby.

Before Herbert's death in 1119, he had probably completed the presbytery with its chapels, the transepts and four bays of the nave. The speed with which the work progressed strikingly demonstrates the vigour of the race of men who built it. The Norman ground plan, which still remains less altered than in any other English cathedral, was typical of its period, with certain local features, such as the very long nave, comparing with those of the neighbouring Ely, Peterborough, and St. Albans, and contrasting with the shorter naves of Durham, Chichester and Gloucester. The high triforium, as high as the side aisles beneath it, compares with our nearer neighbours, whilst it contrasts with the high aisles and low triforia of other

districts. A luxurious feature, still rare in 1101, is the ambulatory or aisle right round the apse, permitting processions to go behind the High Altar.

Herbert de Losinga died on 22 July 1119, and was buried before the High Altar of his cathedral church. His successor, Everard de Montgomery, was enthroned in 1121. It seems likely that the Ancient Throne was brought from Thetford and set up here in time for that event.

Everard appears to have completed the cathedral to the west end and the roof by about 1145. The Norman cloisters and monastic buildings, including the refectory, much of which survives today, were being built about the same time. The tower, the highest Norman tower in England, was probably completed to the level of its interior ceiling by Everard, and finished to the base of the battlements by his successor, William de Turbe, about 1170. It would at first have been crowned by a low timber or possibly stone spire like those in the Rhineland.

Norwich Cathedral Priory

Norwich Cathedral Priory is of outstanding interest, because of the unusually clear evidence it provides of the life lived within it from the 12th to the 16th century. Its activities are recorded in detail in a series of over 3,500 rolls, which, with many other documents extending from 1272 (when previous ones were burnt), to the Dissolution, form the most complete and best preserved collection in England. Its title Priory, rather than Abbey, implies that the real head of the community in a monastic cathedral was the prior (or *First* member), for the bishop, corresponding with the abbot, was mainly occupied with the diocese.

The monks numbered sixty until the gradual decline following the Black Death, and there were, besides, many clerks, squires, and general servants, forming a great and well organised community. Abundant hospitality to rich and poor was an important activity. Maintenance of the community's wide activities cost £2,500 a year – well over £100,000 in today's terms.

Amongst the monks, twelve had special duties. The Master of the Cellar, an office peculiar to Norwich, had a varied responsibility including entertainment of guests and wide activities outside; he had a staff of fifty. The cellarar fed the community; his large staff included a curer of herrings, which presumably came from Yarmouth whose prior had his special lodging in the cloister, next to that of the prior of Lynn; food included 10,000 eggs a week. The sacrist maintained the furnishings of worship; he used 11 hundredweight (558 kg.) of wool annually, and bought cloths from as far apart as Antioch and Aylsham. The precentor led the services and cared for the music and its books. The chamberlain arranged all the clothing on the widest scale. The almoner distributed to the poor, including prisoners, lepers, and

the grammar school boys (not, of course, the grammar school as re-founded by Edward VI); he gave out 10,000 loaves of bread a year. The hostiliar was over the guest hall; the refectorer supervised the refectory or dining hall, and the infirmar maintained the infirmary where the sick monks lay. His purchases included nutmegs, saffron, poppy, fennel, grains of paradise, dyeaquilon, and libanus. The pittancer and communar provided extra allowances of food and drink for feast days. But the monks voluntarily went without these for long periods, to find money to rebuild the

Below and right: (16)
Detail of five bosses from the cloisters. As a full series the cloister bosses have been described as being 'among the finest in the world'.

Far right: (16)
The cloister was built to be full of life – a life which influenced early medieval England as profoundly as her universities today. Before the invention of printing, one walk was the scriptorium or place where monks worked copying books by hand, often illuminating them in gold and colours.

cloister, one of the finest cloisters in the world.

Of the Norman cloister there remain the surrounding walls, with on the south side, considerable remains of the refectory, whose northward windows have since oddly become the southward windows of the library. In a riot of 1272 the citizens burnt the cloisters and did so much other damage that the church had to be re-consecrated on Advent Sunday 1278, in the presence of King Edward I and Queen Eleanor.

The cloister bosses in the vaulted roof form an unrivalled collection. The earliest show leaf forms, oak, hawthorn, wild rose, and grape. From here to the Prior's Door are incidents from the Passion, with the four Evangelists against the east wall. Then, starting from the dark entry and finishing by the locutory door, is a series of a hundred from the Book of Revelation, perhaps the finest series of its kind in the world. They resemble manuscript illuminations of the period, and are easy to identify with the Book of Revelation in one's hand. Subjects include God enthroned, angels and kings worshipping Him, the Lamb slain and triumphant being worshipped, the heavenly orchestra with medieval instruments, the opening of the Seven Seals, the Seven Trumpets, the Four Horsemen, the Seven Vials, the Fall of Babylon, and the Last Judgement. Many other subjects appear also, including a 14th-century windmill at work, the Trinity, and lives of saints. Some amongst many in the north walk, starting from the east, are New Testament incidents from the Resurrection onwards, events such as the Martyrdoms of St. Edmund and St. Thomas of Canterbury, Henry II doing penance for this, and a charter being presented to a monastery.

9

⑩ Medieval Norwich painters produced work comparable with that of Italy. These panels in St. Saviour's Chapel (the chapel of the Royal Norfolk Regiment) came from St. Michael-at-Plea Church. When rector there, Gilbert Thurlow (later Dean of Gloucester), arranged for their restoration, for which the Pilgrim Trust paid £1,000.

The Cathedral Develops

The large
Perpendicular-style
window in the
Bauchon Lady Chapel.
The glass is by Moira
Forsyth (1964), and
depicts some great
Benedictine monks
and saints. William
Bauchon and Dame
Julian of Norwich are
also included.

The cloisters possess many features of great interest. Walking round them from their eastern entrance from the church, we see evidence of their former use. The entrance itself, one of the finest Gothic doorways in England, is called 'The Prior's Door', from the mitred head of Henry de Lakenham, prior 1287–1311, which appears above it. Proceeding along the east walk, we see, in order, book cupboards, some still usable, many blocked; on the stone seat indications of

games once played there; next the blocked entrance to the parlour (the talking place – from *parler*) or treasaunce; then the three arches once leading to the chapter house where daily business was done. Next is the blocked entrance to the dormitory. The door was double, and usually only half opened, as one side only of the step is worn; beyond is the blocked entrance to the former warming house, with the monastery's only fire, beside that of the kitchen. In the south walk are, first the dark entry, formerly leading to the infirmary and prior's hall; beyond these were the granary, the brewery, the water gate now known as Pull's Ferry, whence the stone was brought for the building, and the city. Then a small door which today leads to the library; next, the large door formerly leading to the refectory and kitchen. In the west walk are the lavatorium, where the monks washed, with the gully for water, and arches above for towels; next the guest house doorway, with, above, a boss representing the ever-open door; lastly the door to the locutorium, where visitors were interviewed; this is today the visitors' gift shop, and St. Christopher, carved above it, has become especially appropriate. In the north walk are the entrances to the church, of which the western one is called 'The Monks' Door'.

Returning to the church, we continue the tale of its building. The only large additions made at ground level to the Norman building were the Lady Chapel, 1245–57, and St. Anne's Chapel and the Bauchon Chapel of Our Lady of Pity, built about 1330 and restored as the Chapel of the Friends of the Cathedral, 1968, whilst St. Saviour's Chapel, designed by Sir Charles Nicholson and built in 1930, stands on the site of the Norman St. Saviour's and the later Lady Chapel. The Saxon foundations were discovered on digging its foundations.

Right: ⑥
A general view of the presbytery showing the positions of the ancient throne, the high altar, the choir pulpit and, on the right, the bishop's choir stall.

Below: ⑫
A painting of *The Presentation of Christ in the Temple* by John Opie (1791). This is to be found on the west wall of the Bauchon Lady Chapel.

A disastrous gale in 1362 brought down the spire. In its fall it destroyed the Norman clerestory of the apse. Thomas Percy, bishop 1355–69, brother of the Earl of Northumberland, rebuilt the clerestory on its present splendid scale, giving England the only truly English apse which can rival those of France (Westminster Abbey apse is itself a French design). Though only 85 feet (4.3 metres) high, little more than half the height of Beauvais Cathedral vault, it can stand comparison with its continental rivals because of its perfect proportions. Percy covered it with a timber roof. The nave and transepts were still roofed only with timber, which led to disastrous fires.

Far left: (3)
The bishop's choir stall on the south side of the choir was designed by J.L. Pearson, the architect of Truro Cathedral. It was made in 1895 as a memorial to Bishop John Pelham.

Left: (3)
The pulpit in the choir was designed by J.P. Seddon, the Victorian architect who was responsible for many London churches. It was given in memory of Dean E.M. Goulburn in 1889.

Below: (3)
The choir. The stalls were originally coloured. The organ case, 1950, is a fine example.

The present choir stalls, no doubt re-placing earlier ones, were constructed about 1420 by John Wakering, bishop 1416–25, whose arms are recalled by the hawks on some of the canopies. The misericords are very fine. Then came the great fire of 1463, caused by lightning striking the spire. The nave roof was burnt, and those stalls which stood

under the tower were destroyed. They were reconstructed, with canopies of a different design extending across the transepts, about 1480. Later some more reconstruction was done to them about 1515, after the fire of 1509, in the transepts.

The fire of 1463 necessitated a far greater work – structurally perhaps our finest achievement – the stone vaulting of the nave, carried out by Walter Lyhart, bishop 1446–72. This is a lierne vault, where the main ribs are joined by small ribs crossing from one to another. The bosses at the intersection of the ribs form an exceptionally fine series. From the tower westward they illustrate the Old Testament from Creation to King Solomon, thence the New Testament, to the Last Judgement at the west end. Lyhart also constructed the pulpitum or screen between the nave and choir. The Bauchon Chapel had been vaulted about 1450.

James Goldwell, bishop 1472–99, erected the vault of the presbytery and the flying buttresses outside, to support it. He also built the present stone spire, 315 feet (96 m.) high, the second highest in England. Richard Nykke, bishop 1502–36, completed the vaulting by erecting the transept vaults.

Above: ①
The nave, the so-called people's church, looking east. The main purpose of the nave originally was for processions and to provide a site for additional altars. Today it is used regularly to accommodate large numbers who come to worship in the Mother Church.

Change and Continuity

The Dissolution of the Monasteries in 1538 saw changes, but also here a surprising degree of continuity. The last prior, William Castleton, became the first dean, the monks became canons or minor canons. The offices of organist, precentor, sacrist, singing man, chorister remained, and all these continue today. The Statutes of the New Foundation even provided 'The Common Table of the Ministers', i.e. the monastic refectory continuing in use like a college dining hall. Perhaps the most striking example of continuity was Osbert Parsley. As his monument in the nave states, he became a singing man or lay clerk in the choir in 1535, singing the Latin services; he maintained his position through the Dissolution, the reigns of Edward VI and Mary, and survived through Elizabeth's reign until 1585.

Continuity with the old order is preserved in the office of the Bishop of Norwich in a unique manner. When Henry VIII was dissolving the greater monasteries, he found that the bishop's income would provide him more money than that of St. Benet's Abbey nearby. He therefore appropriated the episcopal endowments, substituted for them the revenues of St. Benet's, and made William Rugg, the last abbot of St. Benet's, bishop of Norwich in 1536. St. Benet's Abbey has never been dissolved, and the bishop of Norwich remains as the one mitred abbot of the old order in England.

The English Prayer Book provided simpler services and ritual. But during the last four centuries, Church music has advanced by steps in their way as impressive as the development of architecture in earlier days. The Statutes of the New Foundation at Norwich provided for six minor canons to sing the services, eight lay clerks 'to be expert in singing', an organist, and eight choristers. No doubt they eagerly acquired and sang the music of each great new composer as

Above: ⑨
The painting of the *Adoration of the Magi* is the work of Martin Schwarz and dates from the 1480s. It is painted on wood, and was probably originally part of a triptych. It forms the altar piece in the Jesus Chapel.

Left: ⑪
The font of the long vanished parish church of St. Mary in the Marsh is the cathedral font. It is an example of a seven sacraments font, once popular in East Anglia. (One sacrament is depicted on seven faces of the bowl and the eighth face shows the crucifixion.)

he came to be known – Byrd, Morley (who may have worked here for a time), Weelkes, Orlando Gibbons, and the rest.

As everywhere in England, there was a sad break in the continuity of Church life during the Rebellion of the 17th century. Joseph Hall, bishop 1641–56, suffered the loss of his property, whilst his description of the sacrilege committed in the cathedral in 1643 has often been quoted. But the cathedral recovered its life speedily at the Restoration. The City Corporation gave the candlesticks on the High Altar; a new organ, parts of which still exist, was erected on the pulpitum, and music recovered its old standard – soon to be enriched by the work of the new composers, Purcell and his successors, and despite the ineptitude of leaders appointed in the 18th and early 19th centuries, the cathedral's life continued to develop.

Left:
This Elizabethan skeleton figure stands within the Norman arcading of the south nave aisle wall and is in memory of Thomas Gooding. It warns passers-by that 'as I am now so shall ye be'.

Far left: ⑤
The transepts, looking north. The roof bosses illustrate: north transept, Jesus' childhood and the Blessed Virgin's life; south transept, Jesus' ministry.

Left: ⑦
The Reliquary Arch houses the Treasury given by the Worshipful Company of Goldsmiths of London in 1972. It was built about 1424 to house relics and to form an ante-chapel to the nearby Reliquary Chapel (now destroyed). There are early 14th-century paintings in the vault.

Below: ②
This monument (attached to the fifth pillar from the west on the north side of the nave) is probably the most interesting in the entire cathedral. It commemorates Osbert Parsley, who served the cathedral as a singing man from 1535–85. This spanned 50 years of profound religious change.

Above: ③
The pelican (not an eagle) lectern in the choir dates from the 14th or 15th century. It is made of latten.

The Cathedral Today

During the modern revival of Church life, the cathedral has been restored and adapted to modern use, and its standard of worship and music greatly improved. It has become truly the Mother Church of its Diocese and justifies its life more strikingly than ever before. Modern transport brings visitors from everywhere and its nave is frequently crowded for special events. Its choir sings superbly and radio and television bring its services into every home. Anyone can gain an intimate relationship with it by joining its 'Friends'. Its treasures are well cared for and new treasures are often given.

Alan Webster, Dean from 1970 to 1978, installed above the western cloister a Visitors' Centre, Coffee and Refreshment Room, Exhibition and Tape/Slide Theatre, showing a guide to the cathedral with its music and a tape for the under-tens, entered by steps adjoining the cathedral shop. In the Exhibition are models of the monastery and ships bringing stone from Caen, reproductions of panels of medieval glass and sculpted stone. The Visitors' Officer's office is also located here.

Paul Burbridge, Dean 1983, re-dedicated St. Catherine's Chapel off the south transept to be a place of quiet – a need greater than ever, when more visitors are welcomed than ever before.

Between 500 and 600 men and women give of their time to the cathedral as guides, welcomers, chaplains, helpers in the shop and buffet, servers, flower-arrangers, sidesmen and many others. Regrettably, there is no provision for the ringing of cathedral bells. Norwich Cathedral is a centre for half a million or so pilgrims and visitors who throng into its doors each year. But above all it remains a strong and constant reminder of the presence of the eternal in a temporal and changing world.